Shadow Work Embroidery
With 108 Iron-On Transfer Patterns

J. Marsha Michler

DOVER PUBLICATIONS, INC.
Mineola, New York

Other Works by the Author
Ribbon Embroidery, 1997, Dover Publications, Inc., Mineola, New York
The Magic of Crazy Quilting, 1998, Krause Publications, Iola, Wisconsin.

Bibliographical Note

Shadow Work Embroidery: With 108 Iron-On Transfer Patterns is a new work, first published by Dover Publications, Inc., in 1999.

DOVER *Pictorial Archive* SERIES

International Standard Book Number: 0-486-40289-4

Manufactured in the United States of America
Dover Publications, Inc., 31 East 2nd Street, Mineola, N.Y. 11501

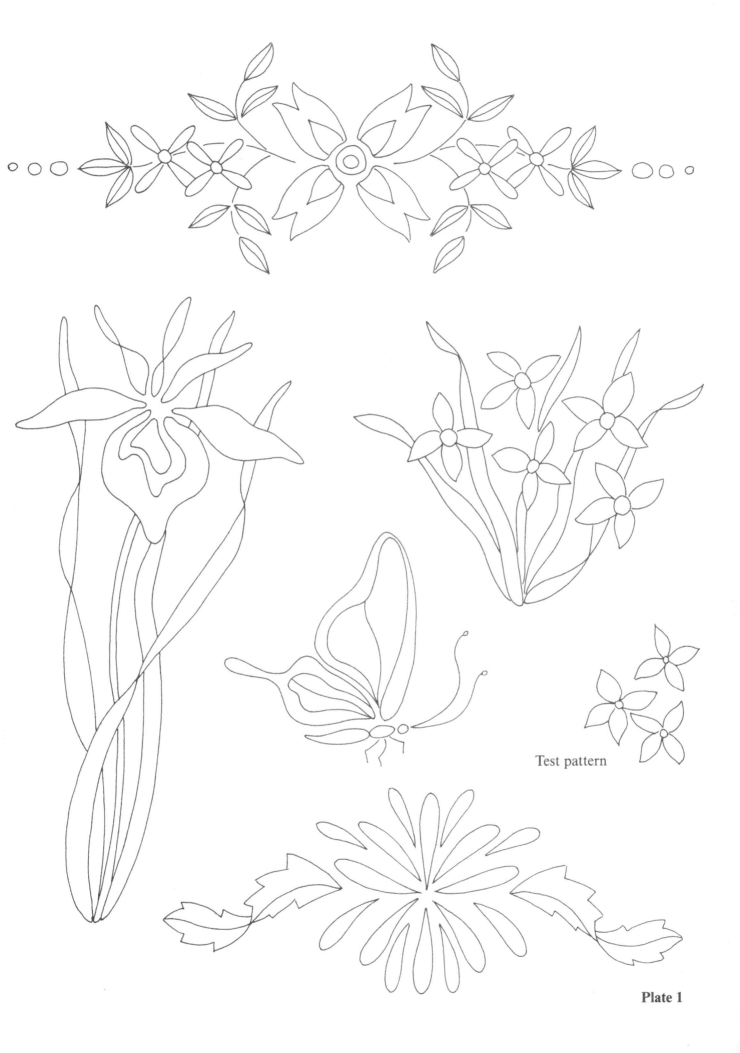

Test pattern

Plate 1

Test pattern

Plate 2

Test pattern

Plate 3

Test pattern

Plate 4

Test pattern

Plate 5

Test pattern

Plate 6

Plate 7

Test pattern

Plate 8

Test pattern

Tea Time

Plate 9

Plate 8

Plate 10

Plate 11

Plate 12

Plate 12

Plate 13

Plate 21

Plate 14

Plate 15

Plate45

Plate 16

Plate 16

Test pattern

Plate 17

Test pattern

Plate 18

Test pattern

Plate 19

Test pattern

Plate 20

Special Instructions for Transferring the Designs

Using a hard lead pencil, lay the fabric wrong side up over the design and trace the lines onto the fabric. Done this way, after embroidery, the design will appear reversed on the front of the fabric. If this is a consideration (it won't matter for some designs), first trace the design onto tracing paper, turn the paper upside down, then trace it onto the wrong side of the fabric.

In other words, the design transferred or drawn onto the back of the fabric should appear backwards. It will then face the right way on the front of the fabric, the same as on the printed page.

Stitches

To begin, leave a tail of about 1", and work the first stitches over and under the tail to secure it. To end a thread, weave the tail through the backs of the stitches without piercing the fabric. It is better to end off threads rather than carry them from one part of a design to another unless the distance is very short. Carried threads will show through to the front.

The **closed herringbone stitch** is worked on the wrong side of the fabric resulting in a double row of backstitching on the front. Learn the stitches by making them about ⅛" in length. As you become comfortable with the stitch, try making them even shorter. With shorter stitches, the area more solidly fills in: the closer the stitches, the deeper the shadow. Stitches can be made longer in narrow areas, and shorter for wider ones. For curved shapes, make longer stitches along the outside of the curve.

Beginning at the upper edge of the area to be embroidered, stitch from B to A. Next, stitch from C to A at the lower edge keeping the thread above the needle. Take the third stitch at the upper edge with the thread below the needle. Continue, working from left to right (reverse the directions if you are left-handed). The stitches will cross each other. Check the right side of the work periodically to be sure that two even rows of backstitch are forming.

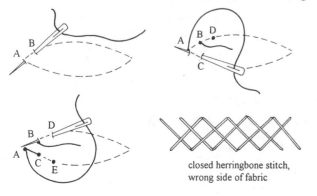

closed herringbone stitch,
wrong side of fabric

The **reverse backstitch** forms a backstitch on the front of the work, and the outline stitch on the back. Take the first stitch from B to A, the second from C to B, the third from D to C, and continue.

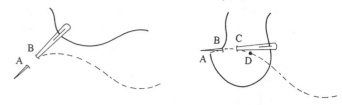

To fill in a circular shape, begin at the left side of the shape making the second stitch touching the first. End with the final two stitches touching each other.

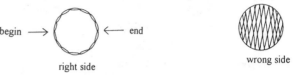

To finish a row that ends in a vertical line, work closed herringbone up to the end, then work reverse backstitch to finish.

To work a leaf that has a central vein, first work reverse backstitch along the vein, then turn and work closed herringbone in the opposite direction.

When a design contains several sections, work closed herringbone in the first section. Then, when working the adjacent section, run the needle under previously made stitches, instead of through the fabric, along one side of the area.

Entire designs can be filled in, or only selected areas of them as in this example of a butterfly.

Notes

Shadow work has traditionally been a part of both white work embroidery and heirloom sewing. Often used in combination with other stitches and techniques, rarely has it been presented as a singular technique, although it easily holds its own. It is unique in creating a shadow-like effect on the fabric. Where light shines through it, the embroidered design appears distinctly. If a piece is lined, or has no light behind it, the design is instead a soft shadow inside of backstitched outlines. It is very easy to do using only two stitches, the Closed Herringbone and Reversed Backstitch. Some uses for shadow work include tablecloths and linens, curtains, clothing, lampshades, and doilies.

If desired, additional stitches may be added to a shadow work design, creating texture, contrast, and intricacy. Some details of a design can be worked in satin or other stitches. French knots may be added to florals, and stems worked in outline stitch.

Some of the designs in this book were inspired by antique or Oriental dishes and pottery. The round designs on Plates 23 and 24 are from antique butter stamps.

Materials and Tools

Semi-sheer fabric is used. All-cotton organdy is a stiffened fabric that is easy to work on, ideal for beginners, and appropriate for many projects. For heirloom sewing, cotton batiste is often used. Some lightweight silks and handkerchief linen are additional choices. Work a small sample in the threads and fabric of your choice before beginning a project. Pre-wash, dry, and press the fabric to prepare for embroidery.

Cotton embroidery floss is commonly used, with one strand for very fine work, or two strands for bolder designs. Other types of flosses may also be used, such as rayon, silk, or metallic. Flower thread may be substituted for two strands of floss. Although traditionally a white-on-white technique, if colors are used they will appear softer when seen through the fabric. Use a working length of thread about one yard long to avoid having to begin and end many times.

Fit the piece to be embroidered into a small hoop, about 4" round. Damage to delicate fabrics can be avoided by first winding the hoop with strips of soft cotton fabric and securing with a few stitches.

Use a size 26 tapestry needle. This type of needle with its blunt point is preferred because the stitches "share" holes in the fabric.

Directions for Using Iron-On Transfers

To use the iron-on transfers, work a test piece in your chosen fabric and thread to be sure the stitches cover the transferred lines. If not, see special instructions below.

Use a natural fabric such as cotton or linen; launder it first, then iron to remove wrinkles.

Many pages have a very small motif printed near an edge of the page which can be used as a test pattern. Before beginning your project, cut out one of these motifs and follow the directions below for making a transfer. If the ink transferred well, go ahead; if not, adjust either the heat or the length of time.

For transferring, use a *dry* iron set at 400°(cotton or linen). Protect the ironing board with an old sheet. To get a stronger impression of the pattern, place a piece of aluminum foil on the board. Place the fabric on the ironing board, wrong side up. Cut out the motif, allowing a margin around the edges. Pin the design to the fabric, printed side down, placing the pins through the margins. Place a sheet of tissue paper over the transfer to protect the iron. Place the heated iron on the transfer and hold down for about 20 seconds. After the transfer has been used, it may be necessary to increase the ironing time for additional transfers. Apply a firm, even pressure to all parts of the design. Do not move the iron across the fabric as this will cause the pattern to blur. Remove one pin and lift one side of the paper to see if the complete design has transferred. If not, replace the pin and repeat the process, concentrating on the area that did not transfer. Do not remove all the pins until the design has been successfully transferred. Then unpin the paper and peel it off. Save the transfer paper to use for additional designs (you can usually get four or more transfers from each pattern) or for reference. You can reinforce vague areas on the fabric with a waterproof felt pen. Make sure that the ink is completely waterproof because just the moisture from a steam iron can cause the ink to run and ruin your work.

Note: Unlike usual iron-on transfers, these are not reversed because they are intended to be placed on the wrong side of the fabric.

Test pattern

Plate 24

Test pattern

Plate 23

Test pattern

Test pattern

Plate 22

Test pattern

Plate 21